Anxiety
Panic Attacks

Trusting God When You're Afraid

Jocelyn Wallace

New
Growth
Press

www.newgrowthpress.com

New Growth Press, Greensboro, NC 27404
www.newgrowthpress.com
Copyright © 2013 by Jocelyn Wallace

All Scripture quotations, unless otherwise indicated, are taken
from the *Holy Bible,* New International Version®, NIV®. Copyright
© 1973, 1978, 1984 by International Bible Society. Used by per-
mission of Zondervan. All rights reserved.

Cover Design: Faceout books, faceout.com
Typesetting: Lisa Parnell, lparnell.com

ISBN-10: 1-939946-25-5
ISBN-13: 978-1-939946-25-6

Library of Congress Cataloging-in-Publication Data
Wallace, Jocelyn, 1976–
  Anxiety and panic attacks : trusting God when you're afraid /
authors Jocelyn Wallace.
    pages cm
  Includes bibliographical references and index.
  ISBN 978-1-939946-25-6 (alk. paper)
 1. Anxiety—Religious aspects—Christianity. 2. Panic attacks—
Religious aspects—Christianity. 3. Fear—Religious aspects—
Christianity. 4. Trust in God—Christianity. I. Title.
 BV4908.5.W34 2013
  248.8'6—dc23   2013018434

Printed in Canada

21 20 19 18 17 16 15 14   2 3 4 5 6

Ryan had to figure out how to keep his boss, George, happy. George seemed to avoid him, and when Ryan did see him, George seemed irritated by everything he did. George was always asking why projects hadn't been done earlier, and then he piled on more work. With only two months until Christmas, Ryan couldn't afford to lose his job. He thought, *How will Cheryl and I be able to afford Christmas presents? Without my job we would certainly lose our house. How would Cheryl and the kids handle that? Would my marriage even survive?*

Ryan couldn't let all that happen—he had to keep this job. He frantically reviewed all of his work—rereading every email his boss had sent him during the past month. He spent the rest of the day trying to work—and worrying about everything that could be wrong. *What if my boss isn't happy with the reports I prepared for the big meeting last week? What if I made a calculation error? What if I end up costing the company thousands of dollars because of my mistake? What if that mistake gets me fired?*

When he got home at the end of the day, he was exhausted. His head was killing him; his muscles were tight; and he could barely focus at supper with his family. Cheryl asked him what was wrong, but all he said was that he'd had a hard day at work. His mind was spinning with anxiety, and he wondered how much more stress he could take. Trying to keep his impossible-to-please boss happy was pushing him to the edge.

* * *

Mia swallowed the lump in her throat and braced herself. She knew what was coming next. She had learned how to handle these episodes at home alone, but now she was in the middle of the grocery store. Her heart was beginning to race, and she was having difficulty breathing. Her mind was racing too, plus her vision was getting blurry. She tried to push her cart quickly to the checkout and get out of the store before things got worse. But the longer she walked, the more she felt like the world was closing in on her. She was so afraid, and she didn't even know why. She felt light-headed. Her heart was pounding, and her fingers and toes were starting to tingle. She wondered if she was dying, or getting ready to have a heart attack, or going insane.

She knew she wasn't going to make it through the checkout, so she ran to the back of the grocery store as quickly as she could. She could barely breathe now. She was seeing stars. She could not feel her hands or feet, and she knew that in about three seconds she was going to start throwing up. She made it to the bathroom just in time. Afterward she sat on the floor, laid her head on her arms, and cried. She wondered, *What is wrong with me? Why am I such a mess? What am I so worked up about?* She sat there crying for fifteen minutes, then slowly got up, left her cart, dragged herself to her car, and drove home. Once home she crawled into bed and slept for three hours. She could not keep living this way. But how could she control her feelings of panic?

Where Does Anxiety and Panic Come From?

Perhaps you can relate to Ryan and Mia, with fears that fill your mind or even the scary experience of a full-blown panic attack. Suffering from anxiety and panic attacks can feel incapacitating. The emotions of fear and panic are so real, so strong, and seemingly so impossible to resolve. Anxiety and panic seem to come out of nowhere. You don't even know what you're thinking, and all of a sudden you're panicking.

The problem starts small, but if unattended, anxiety and panic can affect your whole life. You may feel like you have even become afraid of being afraid. You might begin to worry that you have some rare medical problem causing so many strange physical symptoms.

Before you tackle the problem of dealing with your anxiety, it's important to understand what panic attacks are and how they affect the average human body. Anxiety is defined as "a state of intense apprehension, uncertainty, and fear resulting from the anticipation of a threatening event or situation, often to a degree that normal physical and psychological functioning is disrupted."[1]

That's a bit of a mouthful, but basically it means that you are so fearful or apprehensive of something bad happening that it affects you physically. Sometimes the anxiety may be attached to a particular thought or situation; other times it may not have an obvious connection to anything going on in your life. As anxious thoughts accumulate and anticipated bad results build in your mind, you may feel paralyzed—not knowing what to do or how to handle the situation you are in or the fearful thoughts and feelings that fill your mind. As your anxious thoughts get bigger and bigger, the possible negative results get more and more dangerous. Before long you find yourself panicking because there are no solutions to all of the potential dangers your mind has created. Sound familiar?

When we begin to panic, naturally occurring stress hormones set into motion normal physical processes that may result in our bodies feeling incapacitated as well. God has equipped our human bodies marvelously to be able to handle life. In the event that a dangerous situation crosses our path, our bodies are designed to assess the situation and become ready almost immediately to fight off or run away from the danger. The average, normally functioning human body can be stimulated by the nervous system to become ready to handle an emergency in just seconds. When you are anxious and experiencing apprehension, your body might begin to physically respond to increased feelings of danger. Your mind concludes there is some real threat that must be avoided, but your body cannot figure out what it is because there is nothing physically in front of your eyes demanding your attention. Your mind believes there is some imminent danger and your body is not able to figure out how to handle it, so it shuts down and experiences the physical reaction of the normal functioning of the nervous system when it has been prepped and primed to escape a dangerous threat. In those cases, the full bodily response is called a "panic attack."

A panic attack is defined as "a discrete period of intense fear or discomfort, in which four (or more) of the following symptoms developed abruptly and reached a peak within ten minutes:

- palpitations, pounding heart, or accelerated heart rate
- sweating
- trembling or shaking
- sensations of shortness of breath or smothering
- feeling of choking
- chest pain or discomfort
- nausea or abdominal distress
- feeling dizzy, unsteady, lightheaded, or faint
- derealization (feelings of unreality) or depersonalization (being detached from oneself)
- fear of losing control or going crazy
- fear of dying
- paresthesias (numbness or tingling sensations)
- chills or hot flashes."[2]

This is what Mia experienced when she was in the grocery store, and it left her feeling exhausted and embarrassed. She wasn't sure exactly what had caused the panic attack because she had become so used to thinking in a fearful way. In truth, one small, seemingly harmless thought about how much her groceries would cost quickly spiraled into an illogical worry that she was going to run out of money, lose her house, and ultimately need to file bankruptcy, which was one of her greatest fears. Every time she began thinking about money, strong fears about not being able to take care of herself resulted in a physical experience of panic. When she was at the grocery store, the anxious thought process happened so quickly that she couldn't trace where her fear came from until she calmed down.

Ryan didn't experience the same kind of physical reaction that Mia did, but his anxieties about work took their toll on him physically and relationally as well. Like Mia, his cycle of anxiety began with a stray thought about something that might happen in the future (getting fired by his demanding boss) and spiraled into frantic and ultimately fruitless activity that left him physically and emotionally drained. He is frustrated by his fears, but he can't figure out how to let go of anxiety, be thankful he has a job, and enjoy his family.

God's Cure for Anxiety

You can tell that God understands anxiety when you read in the Bible that anxiety weighs down your heart (Proverbs 12:25). When you're experiencing anxiety, you do feel weighed down. Everything feels heavy, oppressive, incomprehensible, and unmanageable. This is an accurate description of how it *feels* to live without a relationship with God. We are not all-powerful. We are not all-knowing. Without God, our lives *are* scary and out of control because we live in a world where bad things can and do happen. Thankfully, God has designed the perfect cure for anxiety. In Christ, there is a safe place to bring your worries and fears. Christ has paid for the sins that separate you from God and made it possible for you to "approach the throne of grace with confidence, so that [you] may receive mercy and find grace to help [you] in [your] time of need" (Hebrews 4:16). When you trust in Christ for forgiveness, you become a dearly loved child of God (Ephesians 5:1). All the promises in the Bible about how God cares for his children are now your promises. The world can still be a scary place, but when you know God as your heavenly Father and Jesus as your Savior, you can be sure that no matter what, you will be able to turn to God for comfort, help, and protection and he will never desert you.

Many times when fear turns into anxiety we have concluded that God is either not good enough or not powerful enough to stop something from happening that will ultimately harm us. In many cases when we are anxious it is because we have decided that we are the only person we can trust to keep ourselves safe. Ultimately these thoughts frame God as someone who is disconnected from us and not working for our good. But knowing Jesus as your Savior keeps you from being disconnected to God in the middle of your fears. The cross of Christ proves that God is all-loving. He gave his life for you. The resurrection shows you that God is all-powerful—he defeated death. So when you feel anxious and afraid, instead of trying to fight your fearful thoughts on your own, turn toward Jesus. You will find that he is completely trustworthy.

Trusting the God Who Cares for You

The apostle Peter told Christians who were facing suffering to "cast all your anxiety on him [God] because he cares for you" (1 Peter 5:7). Everywhere you look in the Bible, God is giving his people word pictures that describe the ways he cares for his people. According to Psalm 91, God is our refuge and fortress, saving us from our enemies, sheltering us under his wings, and helping us not to fear because he is with us when we call on him. Hebrews 7:25 says that God is able to save those who draw near to him. In Isaiah 40:11 we learn that God takes care of us like a loving shepherd, gathering us in his arms, carrying us close to his heart, and gently leading us. Even through the valleys of the shadow of death we are to fear no evil because God is with us (Psalm 23:4). God really cares about his children! The next time you are full of fear, instead of trying to figure everything out or trying to deal with your fears on your own, turn to the God who cares about you and ask for his help.

Not only do we sometimes fear that God does not care for us or have our best interests at heart, but sometimes we fear that he is not great enough or powerful enough to intervene. Isaiah 40 uses beautiful language to help us understand how much bigger God is than we are, describing him as holding the world in his hand, calling the stars by name, and giving strength to the weary. Next time you are fearful or worried, go outside and look at the stars. Remember that the God who created the stars and knows their names, cares for you.

The greatest cure for anxiety is to learn to trust this God who is good enough to care about your most intricate fear and great enough to deliver you from any evil that might harm you. This does not mean that nothing bad will ever happen to you. But in Christ Jesus, God has taken care of our biggest and most real danger—separation from him (Romans 6:23)—and he's also redeemed our suffering. When you struggle with fear and anxiety, remember that God is with you and for you and that he plans to use your suffering to help you experience his love in even more personal ways (Deuteronomy 8:2–3) while growing you to be more like Christ (Romans 8:28–29).

Seeking God First

Jesus says that God's care for flowers and birds is nothing compared to how well he takes care of us (Matthew 6:25–34). Next time you see a bird, stop and think about how God provides food for it. The next time you see a flower, stop and think about how God provides clothes for flowers. Jesus uses these simple examples to show us that life is about so much more than the things we worry about—like food and clothing or even being taken care of the way we think is best. Jesus tells us to seek God, his kingdom, and his righteousness first and to trust our lives and our troubles to God.

When we are overwhelmed with anxiety, we are usually doing the opposite of this. We are worrying about our lives and concerned that things are not going to turn out right. We try to figure out how to be in charge because we do not trust God to provide what we think is best for us. Instead, we anxiously try to figure out how to take care of ourselves, convinced we know what is best. But even as we do that, deep down we know that we are neither strong enough nor wise enough to figure out life on our own. It is much better to turn toward God and ask him for help.

This is exactly what Peter urges us to do. Just before he says to cast all of our anxiety on the God who cares for us, he calls us to humble ourselves and allow God to be in charge (1 Peter 5:6). Knowing how good God is and that he is able to work out a perfect plan for our lives allows us to throw our anxieties on him, rather than trying to bear them ourselves. We trust that he loves us and will do only what is best for us. Satan's goal is to try to convince us that God is a hoarder, refusing to share and keeping all of the good things for himself. Peter urges us to push against Satan's agenda by humbling ourselves to be willing to receive God's plan for our lives, even if that includes suffering. The passage ends with a reminder that God is all-powerful and has ultimate control over us and our lives both now and forever. We can trust him in the midst of suffering because he "will himself restore you and make you strong, firm and steadfast" (1 Peter 5:10).

As God's dearly loved child, you have access to all sorts of assistance that will help you understand and resolve your anxiety. The Holy Spirit comes to live inside you to empower you for godly living and to help you understand God's Word (Ezekiel 36:27; 1 Corinthians 2:10–13). Jesus himself prays for you at the right hand of God, ensuring that you will be more than a conqueror as you work to sort through your life and follow him in an authentic way. In him you will never be separated from the love of God (Romans

8:34–39). And he has united you with other believers through his death and resurrection so that together you can understand his love more fully and see more clearly how to live it out in the midst of your struggles (Ephesians 2:18).

Getting to the Heart of Your Anxiety

It's not always easy to know what fuels our anxious thoughts. But taking a closer look at the desires, beliefs, and thoughts that underlie your anxiety can help you turn to God more quickly—before you are overwhelmed with the experience of anxiety. What might be underlying your anxiety and fear? It may be scary to think about looking more deeply at the things that make you anxious and fearful. But, remember that, "you did not receive a spirit that makes you a slave again to fear, but you received the Spirit of sonship. And by him we cry, 'Abba, Father'" (Romans 8:15). This is incredibly empowering. Although you may feel like a slave to your fear, in Christ you have been set free and made a child of God. As such, you have the Spirit of God dwelling within you, giving you the power to "take captive every thought to make it obedient to Christ" (2 Corinthians 10:5). As you ask for the Spirit's help, you can take your anxious thoughts captive and bring them under the microscope of God's Word. You will find nothing in them that God has not seen and made provision for in Christ. As you grow in your ability to biblically face the reality of what's in your mind, you will also grow in learning to manage your anxiety in a way that honors God.

Anxiety Points to What You Most Want

Fear is related to desire, so what you fear can tell you a lot about what you most want. For Ryan and Mia, their fears reveal a desire for control, security, and the approval of others. Ryan's fear of his boss's disapproval—and subsequently that he won't be able to provide for his family—has driven him to become an obsessive workaholic, trying desperately to win the approval he believes will ensure his ability to keep his job. For Mia, the fear of not being able to care for herself has caused her to become worried about money, leading to debilitating panic attacks.

There is nothing wrong with Ryan's desire to care for his family or even Mia's desire to take care of herself. But when our desires take center stage in our lives, then we have turned from our trust in God and put our trust where it doesn't belong. Although Mia and Ryan have made their desires more important than God, they are not able to guarantee that those desires will be fulfilled. So they are stuck—wanting something more than God, but knowing that they lack the power to make sure they get what they want. How much better to turn back to the living God—the one who cares for us even more than he cares for flowers and birds.

Ryan and Mia can turn to God in repentance and trust. Because of Jesus, their heavenly Father will freely forgive them and welcome them as his children. You too can turn to Jesus away from anything you have made more important than him. You can ask him for forgiveness and faith. He will help you. Don't be discouraged if you have to do this many times during the day as your fears and desires grip your heart. Jesus will help you as you go to him. With him there is always mercy and grace for your time of need.

Anxiety Points to What You Really Believe

No matter what you say you believe about God and his care for you, your anxiety will highlight what you really, deep-down believe about God. Anxiety is always tied to the belief that something will turn out badly. People do not generally feel anxious about the things they assume will turn out right. Although Ryan and Mia both say they believe in God's goodness and care for them, neither has any sense that God is present in the midst of their circumstances, much less that he is able to provide for them if the worst should happen. Assuming the worst about a given situation is projecting a future where God is neither sovereign nor good. This is essentially unbelief. When you notice that you don't believe that God is with you and going to help you, stop to remind yourself of his true character and presence. Go back to all the descriptions in the Bible of the way God cares for his children. Instead of being full of fear, turn away from your unbelief and ask for the gift of faith. The Spirit will use your repentance to shift your desire for control (and your fear that you don't have it) into a willing submission to God's redemptive plan in your life.

Anxiety Points to What You Really Think

Jesus promised that his death and resurrection makes everything new (Revelation 21:5). This includes our thought life. The apostle Paul calls believers to present themselves to God as living sacrifices, allowing their minds to be made new through the grace that is available in a relationship with Christ Jesus (Romans 12:2). If you struggle with anxiety and fear, then you already know that your thinking has to change. As believers, we are to be thinking more and more about what is good and acceptable to God. Many of the things that are considered during periods of anxiety and panic are not good or acceptable. They are worries and fears that are based on the assumption that God is not all-powerful, not in control, and will not care for you or your concerns the way you want him to. Our anxious thoughts swirl about us and lack an eternal perspective that keeps in mind the glory to which we are being called and for which Christ is preparing us even through our struggles (2 Corinthians 4:16–18).

So how do you take those thoughts captive to Christ? You can start by assessing your thoughts to see if they come from God or from the father of lies. For example, if you are worried about something in the future, ask yourself whether God wants you to worry about your future? (No, he wants you to trust him just for today—Matthew 6:34.) So you can fill your mind with what you know to be true about God: he cares for you; he will never leave you or forsake you. This is how you can turn from being deceived in your thinking (1 Corinthians 3:18) and toward what is true, pure, and honorable (Philippians 4:8). Bring your thoughts to Christ and ask his Spirit to help you discern what is from him and what is not from him. When you notice a lack of trust, ask Jesus for forgiveness and help. Another way to train your mind is to use worship music. Instead of letting the same thoughts cycle over and over in your mind, listen to God's words in music. You can even sing along!

As Ryan began to train his mind to turn away from anxious thoughts and toward Jesus and the truth of his Word, he began to realize that his future did not lie in his boss's hands but in God's. He began to see that he was called to "work at it with all your heart, as working for the Lord, not for men" (Colossians 3:23), trusting God with the results. As his perspective started to shift, he was able to focus better at work and draw more helpful boundaries between his work and the rest of his life. As Mia began to consider how Jesus lived while he was here on earth, she began to see that her desire to take care of herself and not be embarrassed was less important than trusting God. She began to see her anxiety as a reminder of her dependence on God, and she allowed it to teach her humility, accepting that she was not in control of her life.

Practical Ways to Deal with Anxiety

Anxiety and panic are practical problems. You worry about real problems in your real life. If you are going to work at dealing with anxiety you need to apply these biblical truths to specific daily issues. The following are a few areas where you can get started:

Keep Short Accounts

Proverbs 28:1 says that we may be full of anxiety because of unconfessed sin. It is important to keep short accounts of sin and to confess and repent as soon as you become aware that you have handled something in a way that does not honor God. Ryan discovered that much of his anxiety stemmed from how his worry affected his job performance. His worry led him to be distracted and less conscientious in his assignments than he should have been. Guilt over this caused him to fear punishment from his boss. When he confessed this to God and asked for help in overcoming temptation, he began to feel less anxious about losing his job. Mia's fears of spending too much did have roots in overspending in some areas of her life. Guilt over this caused her to fear the instability that could result if her finances weren't in order. As she asked God for forgiveness and wisdom in handling her money, she felt less afraid that her life was going to fall apart and end up in bankruptcy.

Give Control to God (He Is in Charge Anyway!)

Most people who are filled with anxiety struggle with trying to control and manipulate situations to ensure that they will work out in a way that keeps them safe from their perceived dangers. It is important to carefully evaluate how much you are trying to keep things under control and make them fit into your agenda. People tend to get anxious when they think their agenda is in danger of not being fulfilled. When you notice that happening, make your prayer the same one that Jesus prayed in the Garden of Gethsemane, "Not my will, but yours be done" (Luke 22:42).

Pay Attention to Your Internal Questions

More than likely your mind is full of "what if?" questions. Many times "what ifs?" present themselves as certainties, but they are really only projections of what might happen in the future. And the future in view is rarely one where God's mercy and grace is on display. Instead it's a hopeless future where God is not present and active. Notice when you are beginning to follow a line of thought that leads down this path. If your thinking leads you to hopelessness and despair, you can be sure you have left out God and are pursuing sinful anxiety. Ask yourself questions about your thoughts. Your "what if?" thoughts have the capacity to help you figure out what you are truly anxious about. Use these thoughts to help you see where your desires, beliefs, and thoughts have gone astray. Go back to the Bible passages about who God is and how he cares for you. Remind yourself that only God knows the future, and he has promised that your future will always include his presence and help.

Focus on Growth during the Calm Moments

Refocusing your mind is not easy when you're in the middle of anxiety or a panic attack. So it is important to be training your mind during moments of peace. God designed us to think clearly and to have sound judgment even when the situation is scary or dangerous; we can think under stressful or perplexing situations. Even under the curse of sin and with the long-term effects of sin on our minds and bodies, we are able to think, reason, and train our bodies and minds to function in a way that is righteous, helpful, and wise (Romans 6:12–14).

One of the easiest ways for you to evaluate your thoughts is to write them all down. One way to help yourself grow is to keep a "thought journal." Once you have written down your anxious thoughts, you can start to learn and apply biblical solutions. Even a week of doing a thought journal will help you see patterns. It may feel awkward at first to think about thinking. But once you begin to observe thought patterns, you will notice how something you were thinking about resulted in feelings of dread, nervousness, apprehension, hesitation, uncertainty, fear, distress, or alarm.

Use your thought journal to help you understand what desires, beliefs, and thoughts trigger anxiety. Once you are able to perceive what the true problems are, use Scripture and wise counsel to plan ways to solve them. Anxiety develops because we do not know solutions to problems and feel like there is no one to trust who does know. God has the best solutions to all problems. Learn to rely on the Bible for authoritative answers to your real-life problems. This will be difficult without help from trusted people in your life. Identify wise, godly friends who can help you think through your struggles. Ask others to pray for you. You don't have to tell everyone you know about your struggles with anxiety, but you can share your burdens with a few people you trust to pray with and for you. You may also want to consider meeting with your pastor or a biblical counselor.

Don't forget to look for ways to help and serve others. It is possible that your anxiety keeps you paying such close attention to yourself that you are becoming self-centered. When you serve someone else, you focus your energy outside yourself. Obviously, this is not a replacement for solving the problems, but it will help you build a new life centered less on worry and more on loving God and others (Matthew 22:36–40).

Take Care of Your Body

There are true physical components to anxiety and panic attacks. If you learn to take care of your body when it is full of anxiety, you will likely have a better ability to keep yourself from going into a full panic attack. Notice when your body gives you warning signs that you are thinking anxious thoughts without even realizing it. Pay attention to instances when you become jumpy, clammy, or have an anxious stomach. Allow those symptoms to help you become aware of any stray anxious thoughts that need to be dealt with. Try to slow down to see what was happening before you started to feel anxious. This will help you dig at the roots of your anxiety and stop the panic cycle before it begins. When you are convinced you are in danger, hormones will start pumping through your body to prepare it to either fight or run away.

Even as you turn away and give Jesus your anxieties and fears, you may find that it takes a while to help your body relearn to handle fear. It has been habitual to react immediately, and you will need to relearn to function. In the meantime you may experience jitteriness, frequent bathroom trips to relieve yourself, or the occasional upset stomach. Those symptoms are likely to decrease as you learn to handle stress and anxiety in a biblical way, but even if the symptoms don't go away altogether you can learn to trust that God is with you.

It may sound basic, but another good way to take care of your body is to breathe slowly and deeply when you are anxious. When you feel a panic attack coming on, learn to stop and breathe slowly and deeply. Many physical symptoms are either caused or aggravated by oxygen deprivation—which is caused by quick shallow breathing when panicking. Lie down on the ground, elevate your legs, and focus on taking long, slow deep breaths that fill your lungs. Take the time to get your breathing under control, to get enough oxygen into your system, and then allow your mind to face whatever thought of anxiety might have triggered such a panic reaction.

You might want to consider getting a physical. Having a panic attack *feels* as you might imagine a heart attack feels. Many times panic attacks are mistaken for more serious or life-threatening medical situations. If you feel the physical symptoms listed at the beginning of this minibook, it is important to have a physician investigate to be sure there are no serious underlying medical conditions.

Learning to handle anxiety and panic can be a huge blessing. There are many causes behind fear, worry, anxiety, and fretfulness. As you deal with anxiety and panic, be confident of what Psalm 34 says about God. The psalmist says that the eyes of the Lord are toward the righteous and his ears are open to their cry. When the righteous cry out to God, he hears and delivers them out of all their troubles. He is near to the brokenhearted and saves those who are crushed in spirit. Because you have a loving heavenly Father, you can expect your cries for help to be heard and you can expect to be delivered from the anxieties that have taken over your life.

Endnotes

1. "Anxiety," Dictionary.com, The American Heritage® Stedman's Medical Dictionary (Houghton Mifflin Company), http://dictionary.reference.com/browse/anxiety (accessed: November 27, 2012).

2. American Psychiatric Association (2000), Diagnostic and Statistical Manual of Mental Disorders, rev. 4th ed. (Washington, DC: Author).

Simple, Quick, Biblical

Advice on Complicated Counseling Issues
for Pastors, Counselors, and Individuals

MINIBOOK
CATEGORIES

- Personal Change
- Marriage & Parenting
- Medical & Psychiatric Issues

- Women's Issues
- Singles
- Military